A Dustbin of Milligan

A DUSTBIN
OF MILLIGAN

by

SPIKE MILLIGAN

Author of
SILLY VERSE FOR KIDS

LONDON: DENNIS DOBSON

First published in Great Britain in 1961 by
Dobson Books Ltd., 80 Kensington Church Street, London, W.8

Printed in Great Britain by
Clarke, Doble & Brendon, Oakfield Press, Cattedown, Plymouth

Contents

POLITICS AND OTHER NONSENSE

FAIRY TALES

Poems

Porridge

Why is there no monument
    To Porridge in our land?
If it's good enough to eat
    It's good enough to stand!

On a plinth in London
    A statue we should see
Of Porridge made in Scotland
    Signed "Oatmeal, O.B.E."
        (By a young dog of three)

Bazonka

Say Bazonka every day
That's what my grandma used to say
It keeps at bay the Asian Flu'
And both your elbows free from glue.
So say Bazonka every day
(That's what my grandma used to say)

Don't say it if your socks are dry!
Or when the sun is in your eye!
Never say it in the dark
(The word you see emits a spark)
Only say it in the day
(That's what my grandma used to say!)

Young Tiny Tim took her advice.
He said it once, he said it twice
He said it till the day he died
And even after *that* he tried
To say Bazonka! every day
Just like my grandma used to say.

Now folks around declare it's true
That every night at half past two
If you'll stand upon your head
And shout Bazonka! from your bed
You'll hear the word as clear as day
Just like my grandma used to say!

12

Lady B's Fleas.

Lady Barnaby takes her ease
Knitting overcoats for fleas
By this kindness, fleas are smitten
That's why she's <u>very</u> <u>rarely</u> bitten.

"Gentlemen – a clue – this man recently had his trousers in the press."

SH

Why ?

American Detectives
Never remove their hats
When investigating murders
In other people's flats.

P.S.   Chinese Tecs
Are far more dreaded!
And they always appear
bare-headed!

16

The people who live
   on the Oojah-ka-Piv
Stand around in bundles of nine*

When asked how it feels
   they reply 'Curried Eels'!
Otherwise – everything's going fine!

* 9

SM

Mrs. Dighty

Mrs. Dighty
In her nightie
Walking in the dark

Trod upon
A puppy dog's tail
And made the creature bark

Mrs. Dighty
In her nightie
Let the puppy go

By lifting up
   her instep
And raising her
   big toe.

Holes

Mountains should have holes in
  To see to the other side.
By observing the view thru this aperture
  Would save a considerable ride.

So Fair Is She

So fair is she !
So fair her face
So fair her pulsing figure

Not so fair
The maniacal stare
Of a husband who's much bigger.

Illness Is Good For You

One good appendicitis—

Or a cure for St. Vitus dance

Pays for a Harley Street Surgeon's

Vacation in the South of France.

'Tis due to pigeons
that alight
On Nelson's hat
that makes it white.

NOTHING.

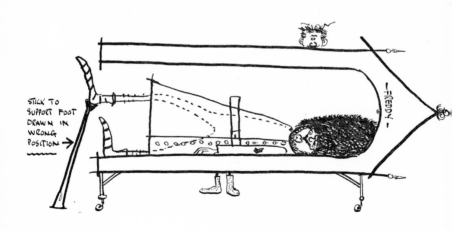

STICK TO
SUPPORT FOOT
DRAWN IN
WRONG
POSITION →

← FREDDY →

Soldier Freddy
was never ready,
But Soldier Neddy,
unlike Freddy
Was _always_ ready
and steady,

That's why,
When soldier Neddy
Is-outside-Buckingham-Palace-on-guard-in-the-
pouring-wind-and-rain-
being-steady-and-ready,
Freddie —
is home in beddy

Area of Scofflufus

Area of Scofflufus

UNEATABLE

S.H.

Scorflufus

By a well-known National Health Victim No. 3908631

There are many diseases,
That strike people's kneeses,
Scorflufus! is one by name
It comes from the East
Packed in bladders of yeast
So the Chinese must take half the blame.

There's a case in the files
Of Sir Barrington-Pyles
While hunting a fox one day
Shot up in the air
And *remained hanging there!*
While the hairs on his socks turned grey!

Aye! Scorflufus had struck!
At man, beast and duck.
And the knees of the world went Bong!
Some knees went Ping!
Other knees turned to string
From Balham to old Hong-Kong.

Should you hold your life dear,
Then the remedy's clear,
If you're offered some yeast—don't eat it!
Turn the offer down flat—
Don your travelling hat—
Put an egg in your boot—and beat it!

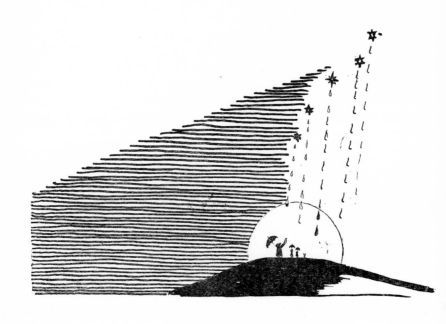

Rain

There are holes in the sky
Where the rain gets in,
But they're ever so small
That's why rain is thin.

Stories

Fretwork, the Shame of our Cities

Fretwork, the Shame of our Cities

Hercules "Fred" Bleriote snuggled down in his favourite chair. He was a tall man, as you, dear reader, will notice when he stands up. Hercules puffed casually on his cherry-wood samovar, a wisp of smoke escaped from the bowl, he immediately inserted a fresh wisp. Lazily he drew on his pipe, he drew on the wall, the ceiling, the soles of his boots, was there no end to this man's ability?[1]

The time was 6.30 and France was at war. To all outward appearances he was at peace, but a quick X-Ray shows his inward appearance differed drastically. (Just hold this page up to the light, you'll see what I mean.) Hercules was in a state of acute agitation, on the table before him lay a freshly opened letter which he was even *now* freshly reading. . . . "Your mistress Madame Legerts (if you pronounce that right, it should sound like 'My dam leg hurts' : this is a desperate attempt to make you laugh) is in our hands, do not tell the police or she will meet a fate worse than death. (For the love of him Hercules could not think of a fate worse than death.) Wrap ten million francs around a brown paper parcel, stand on top of the Sacré Coeur, and sing the third act of Rigoletto."

Hercules clutched the back of his forehead, he reeled forward, he reeled backwards, he reeled sideways, and finally reeled upright. A sudden second sense told him danger was nigh. With one tigerish bound he leapt behind the fire screen, not a moment too soon. A mere eight hours later a brick

[1] Yes there was.

landed on the very spot he had vacated. I should like to mention that a brick also hit him the moment he leapt behind the fire screen. He grabbed the phone: "Le Police" he gabbled in fluent French. In a matter of seconds the Maria Noire was knocking at the door; out sprang a tall handsome cross-eyed Gendarme followed by trente-deux (34) French policemen, who immediately gesticulated in a corner. They advanced on Hercules, led in the middle by a short bearded detective, wearing the uniform of a plain clothes detective. He doffed his hat, teeth, gloves, boots and fired a pistol in the air. "We are Le Police," he said with an air of authority. "Thank heaven you've arrived," cried Hercules. As one man the police looked heavenwards and exclaimed, "Thank you heaven." It was 6.32 and France was at War. Hercules pointed towards a direction, "Come in, make yourselves at home," They accepted the invitation and in a trice, several were in the garden drinking wine, two were upstairs sleeping softly with the blinds drawn, the rest sat around the house hitting each other and making little raffia mats. It was now 7.00 and France was at *War!*

CHAPTER II

A Race to the Death and back again with only one Tea Break!

Next morning, the bearded detective appeared on the landing wearing Hercules' best dressing gown. "Quelle belle Jour," he announced. After breakfast of frogs and porridge, he cornered Hercules. "Why are you keeping us all a prisoner in your own house?" Hercules blanched blanche, he advanced on the bearded Detective and thrust the ransom note under his nose. "Why did you thrust that note under your nose?" asked the detective. "It's not under my nose, it's under yours, it's the way this story's written that makes it confusing." (How dare he! That's the last time he's in a story of mine—Signed Spike

Milligan). . . . The bearded detective read the ransom note, "*Sacré bleu,* this note is no concern of ours, it's addressed to you."

"But M'sieur Detective, I phoned you because I was in trouble."

"What a nerve, when we're in trouble, do we phone you? Huh, no m'sieur, this is a job for the police." And by God dear reader so it was, join the police and help. It was now 4.40 and France was at war!

Author's Note: I know this story lacks that vital something, but what the hell.

S.M.

The Great Man

My Uncle Bertram Twitt was a great man. He told me so himself. One can't argue with facts like that. He was a tall, handsome, cross-eyed man with eczema. He walked with a pronounced limp, L-I-M-P, pronounced "limp". I was five at the time. Uncle Bertram was plagued with a bald head. It happened when he was twenty-one. "I was wounded in the head whilst fighting Turko-Arab forces in Mesopotamia, and my hair fell out," he told me. Latterly I discovered that he went bald naturally, but that was too ordinary for a great man. Hope came to him when the family were living in Poona. Uncle Bertram was approached by a Mr. Panchelli Lalkaka, a Hindu Holy man. For ten rupees, he guaranteed to cure my Uncle's bald head of baldness. The treatment involved my Uncle sitting naked in a darkened room, with a mixture of cow dung, saffron and treacle spread on his head. "Stay in there three days sir," said the Holy man.

It didn't work. My Uncle hit the Holy man with my brother's christening mug. I was now seven. My Uncle took to wearing a toupée. One day my Uncle said, "Nephew, Nephew, there are many wicked landlords in this world, come, I must teach you to shoot." He thrust a great Mauser Rifle at me. He put me in a bush overlooking a dried up Monsoon lake. He ran from boulder to boulder, and I fired blank cartridges at him and he returned the fire with an old Arab Pistol. Now the crows and hawks of India are much angered by rifle fire, which is usually directed at them. They took to diving on my Uncle. As he disappeared behind a rock a great hawk dived after him. It reappeared, clutching something in its talons. Uncle appeared a second later revealing a clawed bald head, and swearing above and beyond the call of normality. He threw rocks, sticks, clods, one of his shoes and discharged his pistol, but the hawk flew beyond the reach of the great man. That evening, wearing a handkerchief knotted around his heavily iodined head, he wrote a letter to England ordering a fresh wig and a powerful adhesive glue. For days after, he roamed the countryside with a pair of binoculars and a ladder. He searched every hawk's nest for fifty square miles around, but alas, never again did he find that wig, and never again did we play at shooting. Years later an Indian naturalist reported a strange find, a hawk's nest made from a wig; stranger still it wasn't my Uncle's. I was eleven at the time.

The White Flag

The two great Generals and the two great Armies faced each other across one great battlefield. The two great Generals marched about their two great Armies as they faced each other across one great battlefield. One great General said to himself, "We can't hold out against this other great Army much longer," and the other great General said, "We can't hold out against this other Army much longer," so the first great General said to one of his great Sergeants, "Hoist a white flag," and the second great General said to his great Sergeant "Hoist a white flag."

Private Fred Lengths was commanded by one great General to haul up the flag. At the same time, Private Norrington Blitt had also been signalled by his General to hoist their white flag, and so the two great Armies stood surrendering to each other across the battlefield. It was very quiet, and the two white flags were the only movement seen.

Three days passed, and one great General said "What's happened?", as did the other great General. Both great Generals were informed that each side had surrendered to the other. "Impossible," said the first General.

"It can't be true," said the second General.

"My arms are aching," said Private Blitt, as did Private Lengths.

"How long have they had their flag up?" said the first great General.

"Three days," at which time the second great General had asked the same question, and received the same answer.

"Tell them *we* surrendered—*first*!"

The message was shouted across the great battlefield.

"No, no," was the reply, "*We* surrendered first." Neither side wanted to lose the initiative. Stalemate.

The two great Generals met in a tent in the middle of a field. "According to my notes," said the first, "our flag went up at one minute to eleven on the 1st April."

"So did ours," was the reply.

"But," said the first General, "I gave the order to put the white flag up at a quarter to eleven. . . ." and was met with the same reply. Stalemate II.

The first General screwed his eyes up, screwed his knees up, his nose, teeth and ears. "Tell you what—my peace flag is whiter than yours."

"Nonsense," was the furious reply. "Hold ours up to the light—not a stain in sight. We use the new Bluinite."

"Bluinite!" guffawed the facing General. "My dear fellow, Rinso, the new white Rinso, is my answer to you. That's why I say my flag is whiter."

"The window test!" they said simultaneously.

In due course, a window was brought, against which the two flags were held. Alas, both were of the same degree of white intensity. Stalemate III.

Meantime, the makers of Bluinite and Rinso had heard of the conflict.

"You aren't going to let that lot get away with it," said the Managing Director of Bluinite to the first General, at which time, as you can guess, Sir Jim Rinso was inciting the second General.

"I will prove who surrendered first," he said, as the first great atomic blast exterminated them.

(Traditional)

The Violin

It could only happen once in a lifetime. It happened to Joseph Schilkraut. In the Commercial Road, his pawnshop was the sole survivor in the district of wholesale shut-downs during the 1930 depression.

"There ain't no more money left in the world," he told his wife at breakfast. "Nobody *ever* redeems their pledges these days. Look at the stuff I got in the shop! I can't get a penny for any of them, ach! There just *ain't no more money.*"

A host of pawned clocks chimed ten from the shop. In the good old days he would have been opened at eight-thirty sharp, but now, there was no point.

He finished his tea, and pulled the shop blinds. It was cold. The windows unseeing with condensation he wiped clear.

Across the road, outside the Labour Exchange groups of grey, cold, unemployed men stood talking. Some wore Army medals—"Poor fellers," thought Joe.

Farther down the street some had started a fire with orange boxes.

The day passed without a customer.

"I suppose," thought Joe, "people ain't got anything to pawn any more!"

It was the shortest day. At four he lit the gas: its light bathed the room in a sea of sepulchral green.

"Ach, might as well close," Joe muttered. But what was this? Someone coming in! Yes ... Yes, he was.

The shop door opened, an elderly man made a shuffling entrance.

"You still open, mate?"

Joe shrugged his shoulders. "Well—mmm, yes. What you got then?"

The old man held up an army sandbag. "Do you give anything on musical instruments, mate?"

Joe winced. "Instruments?" He pointed to a host of trumpets that festooned the walls. "You can see how much I need instruments."

The old man stood silent—his great shabby overcoat hung from his stooped shoulders like tired wings.

"Oh, all right." There was a note of pity in Joe's voice. "What you got?"

The old man laid the sandbag on the counter. "It's a fiddle, mate," he said, sliding it from the bag.

At first glance Joe could see it was old, very old. He took it behind the counter under the light and peered into the "f" holes. The floor of the instrument was thick with dust. All the while the old man stood silent.

"Won't keep you long," said Joe, removing the dust with a paint brush. *Nicolo Amati. 1604.*

Joe polished his glasses and looked again—*Nicolo Amati. 1604.* That was what the label said.

Steady, Joe, there's a million fakes floating about. This could be another, except, this didn't *feel* like a fake. The label was vellum, and the signature in faded brown ink. Joe had a strange feeling come over him. The old man stood waiting. Joe showed no outward emotion.

"Is it worth *any*thing?" asked the old man.

Joe laid the violin on the sandbag, took off his glasses.

"I don't know, sir. Leave it here a day or two and I'll let you know!"

The old man took a pace forward. "A *day* or two?—I was hopin' I might get somethin' right away, mate. See I'm skint and hungry—bleedin' hungry. Couldn't you let me have a couple o' bob on account? I mean, it *must* be worth more than that."

Joe put the violin into the sack.

44

"All right—two bob."

The old man took the coin. "Good luck," he said spitting on it, and shuffled from the shop.

Heart beating, Joe bolted the shop door. He took the stairs to the loft two at a time. He pulled down his Lexicon of "Violins—Viols and Cellos."

For an hour he compared the violin against illustrations. Measurements, wood, scroll—all signs pointed in favour. There was one person who could tell him for sure—Uncle Alfred!

Eight minutes later, the phone rang in Uncle Alf's shop.

"Hello, Alfred Bloom's Antiques here."

The babbling voice of nephew Joe came racing over the phone. He told all.

"You got to come down now and verify it, or I won't sleep."

"Me come down now? I'm in Leeds remember?"

"Leeds, Schmeeds, this could mean a fortune—you can have your cut."

"I'll be down on the night train."

At six-fifty the following morning Uncle Alfred was in the shop. Without even letting him remove his hat or coat, Joe pushed the violin at him. Screwing an inspection glass in his eye, Uncle Alf roamed the body of the old violin. The glass dropped from his eye, he started to shake.

"Joe—it's real," he said. "It's an Amati! Worth forty thousand pounds anywhere in the world."

The two men stood silent in the room. Then Joe started to speak.

"Forty thousand pounds," he kept repeating.

"And that's putting it at a minimum," interjected Uncle Alf.

Joe fell back into his chair. This meant the start of a new life—no more penny pinching, no more bargaining, anti-semitism, bills, arguments, sleepless nights, rent. All over, all over. He started to cry. . . .

Uncle Alf was speaking: "You ain't told me where you got it."

"An old feller came in—I give him two bob deposit."

"*Two* bob," Uncle Alf clapped his hands. "Then he don't know the value. We're home and dry, ha ha!"

Joe held up his hand. "Just a minute—he's entitled to a slice of the money—it's his violin."

Uncle's face dropped.

"You mad, Joe?—Who found out it was worth forty thousand? Him? No—it was *you* and *me*. No son, that's the luck of the game—offer him two quid—and later— send him an anonymous hundred. He'll be happy. Come on, now, wake up! Business is business!—He'd do the same to you——"

A day went by, two, three, a week—the old man never appeared. Joe and his wife were taking sleeping pills. Late one January evening, the old man came.

"Sorry I been so long," he coughed. "I been ill wiv the flu. I lives on me own so I di'n' get much attention."

There was a pause. Joe waited for the man to ask the question. He did.

"Er—did you make up yer mind about the fiddle?"

Joe drew a deep breath. "Yes," he exhaled. "I have."

'Thank God, I needs a few bob—huh."

"I'll give you two quid for it."

At the mention of money the old man swayed.

'Two quid?" he echoed.

"Yes."

"Oh." He stood blinking in the middle of the room. "I fought it might be worth a bit more."

Joe laughed. "More? How much you reckon it's worth, then."

The old man gave Joe a steady gaze. "Forty thousand pounds," he said. . . .

The Referee

(A brief recountment)

Hannigan's dad, was a boxing referee, he refereed boxing matches. The fact he was a confirmed alcoholic produced some startling decisions.

"MacFunn is the winner," he announced, pointing to a broken, unconscious figure on the canvas.

All hell broke loose, the ring erupted in a sea of flailing managers and seconds. "What the hell do you think you're doing?" howled the loser's manager.

"Now then," cautioned Hannigan's dad. "Your man lost on a foul, MacFunn was sneezing when he got hit," so saying he fell down under the weight of alcohol.

There was the Dick Panther versus Killer Blinn affair. The first round was murder. Blinn was hit thirty-seven hundred times, six of these by Hannigan's dad. As the gong sounded for the end of the round, Hannigan's dad shouted "Fight on," and insisted on twelve more seconds of fight.

"Injury time," he announced. An apple core bounced off his head. "The Queen," he shouted, stood to attention and fell sideways like a felled ox.

Despite this, he worked regularly, in third-rate halls, mainly because he was third rate. However, he started to gain a peculiar notoriety, whereas, at one time, bets were on the pugs, betting was now transferred to Hannigan's dad, as to what kind of decision he would make. It got so that people just waited for the end of the bout for the real fun to start. His popularity shot up to a peak when, one night, he disqualified both contestants and declared himself the winner.

Boxing Czar Zoltzman saw a chance to use him.

"Stake him a thousand nicker to tell us who's going to get the decision."

Hannigan's dad perused the pile of one pound notes on Zoltzman's desk. "O.K.," he said. "Nikky Lewis is going to win in the heavyweight contest."

At the fight, Hannigan's dad was found in the bar. Never had he had so much money, and never had he had so much drink. Two men carried him into the arena on a stretcher, tumultuous applause greeted him, the boxers entered in comparative silence. While consulting the timekeeper, Hannigan's dad fell through the ropes; reaching out to save himself, he inadvertently pulled the bell cord. Out came the two boxers and set to in their dressing gowns.

"Whoa back," shouted Hannigan's dad reappearing. He beckoned the men to the centre of the ring, pulled their heads down, produced a cigar. "Either of you bums got a light?" he said, reeling with laughter.

The first round was noticeable for Hannigan's dad circling the boxers and singing "In my dear little Alice blue Gown." The crowd was only too eager to join in.

Round two saw him staggering dangerously near the fighters. Kerthungggg! a great loping right from Nikky Lewis

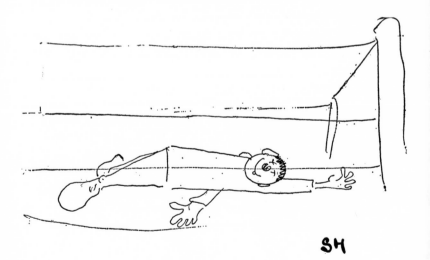

SH

sent Hannigan's dad staggering, he seemed to go down, but no! shaking his head he flayed into the two amazed pugs and sent Nikky Lewis unconscious to the canvas, only to be caught in turn by the remaining, now infuriated boxer.

Down went Hannigan's dad. He stayed down. He died. "Alcoholic poisoning" was the Coroner's verdict. The strangest verdict to any fight.

Letters to Harry Secombe

I

Hello—Meagan Secombe! Sorry I haven't written before but I've been sea-sick. Gad, it's hot. Male passengers are going mad with the heat! With my own eyes I actually saw an Englishman *unbutton his dinner jacket at dinner*! He has since been certified. Gad, it's hot. The walls of the cabins pour with a steaming humid liquid vapour. Around us is the Red Sea, a festering green sheet of unskimmed molten brass. You can grab a handful of air and squeeze the sweat out of it.

Ah! but there's always the swimming pool. Lad! have you ever considered the spectacle of two thousand passengers, all jammed in a swimming pool made for twenty. They've been packed in there for three days now, and we can't get 'em out. We've managed to extricate one lady by pouring cokernut oil over her and prising her up with a crowbar, which gave her the effect of looking like an aged Venus rising from the sea.

Gad, it's hot. At two this morning one of the crew went berserk! Overcome with the heat he ran amok with his teeth out, shouting "Eastbourne for ever, Eastbourne, pearl of the West!" and then proceeded to swallow pieces of cardboard with the word "ice cube" written on it. To keep him quiet, I kept hitting him on the head with a piece of cardboard on which was written the word "sledgehammer". It was a night of real fun. Unfortunately the heat victim aroused several passengers by sliding the word "noise" under their cabin doors. One annoyed passenger appeared in the corridor naked, save for a gladiator's helmet and a pair of corsets, and shouted "Quiet please, we're not *all* mad you know" and threw himself over the side. As he floated aft, he shouted, "Help, drop me a line." "All right," I said, "What's your address?[1]" As he went down for the third time, he bellowed, "I want my money back." It was great fun next day auctioning off his effects. It's homely fun like this that makes us the great seafaring people we are.

This is really a first-class modern ship. The most interesting thing is the brass plate on the deck, saying "Nelson fell here." I'm not surprised. I fell over it myself.

Went to bed early, and, by sleeping at full speed, I managed to reach dawn ahead of the ship. The sun rose on the starboard side today. (The skipper turns the ship around each day so we all get a turn at it.) Looming in the morning mists are the great Volcanic Isles of Itfiflan, behind which lies Aden.

So that we could take photographs and oil paintings, the Captain ran the ship close inshore. He is a great sailor and navigator. Only a man with a great knowledge of the sea could take a ship so close inshore.

0800: All passengers in the sea helping push the ship off sandbank. Through a porthole the Captain, now purple with apoplexy, is shouting instructions and offering money prizes if we can re-float her before anyone spots us. All the crew stand at the rails shouting encouragement. What nice fellows they are. By mid-morning we had her afloat, and we sat down to a combined breakfast and lunch. Curried porridge and chips, fried fish with rice krispies. The Purser has a motto, "Eat as much as you can, folks. You pay for it. The more you eat, the cheaper you travel." I left a Scotsman trying to eat enough to enable him to travel free.

Slowly the great s.s. *Arcadia* steamed into Aden Harbour. Astern I saw a silver-white flash in the water, and the maw of a great shark as he gulped down some ship's waste. An old man saw it. "Shoo, go away naughty fish," he shouted. I learned later that he kept chickens in his cabin and was

[1] A joke.

54

worried about them. As we neared the shore the water became a mass of oil and it smelt something awful. The glare of the sun was immense. I said to the First Officer, "Gad, that sun's hot," to which he replied, "Well, you shouldn't touch it."

After lunch we descended the gangplank to the launch. At last I was to step on a part of the British Empire! Last time I was in Aden in 1933 it was just a dirty hot coaling station. Today it is just a dirty hot coaling station. Ashore the only thing that had changed was the ice-cream paper I had thrown in the gutter in 1933. It had grown older. A long thin Yemini taxi driver beckoned us to his long thin taxi. "We got Abada-bar yaba dada doo, England very good man, how do you yardi boo." "Ying tong iddle i po," I replied, and that settled it. Away we drove out towards the crater. There we hit the Arab caravan halting places. Everywhere there were miserable wretches moaning "Buckshees." Later I discovered they were all the tourist passengers off the ship. We saw one or two camels, and got their autographs on our shoes.

I got a lot of wonderful snaps of our ship as seen from the shore, the British soldiers on guard outside the British barracks, and the Union Jack over the port. What fun I'll have showing the people back home photos of the mysterious Occident. I shook hands with a friendly Arab . . . I still have my right hand to prove it. Nevertheless, everywhere are signs of organized British rule . . . all those happy fights in the café. We had a bomb explosion the day we were there. Of course, the café proprietor charged us extra for it. Those happy greetings that hang from every window "Tommy go home." In the harbour, with its guns trained on the shore, was the *H.M.S. Cambia* on a friendly visit. From the Yemen hills beyond came happy sounds of rifle fire. We were informed by the recruiting sergeant that we could partake in the fun if we signed "this little bit of paper and put on this uniform." As our launch headed back to the ship I couldn't help feeling we were getting out just in time. My suspicions were confirmed when, training my binoculars on the Governor's Palace, I could see him packing furiously, and his wife ironing a white flag.

Goodbye dear Neddy! my next report will be to describe the attacks of Arab Dhows as we sail from the shore.

Love to Myra,

Regards,

SPIKE.

II

Hello, Ned—dear lad!

We left Aden on the evening of April 19th. The sun was setting, and Ned lad! the sunsets in this part of the world are almost miraculous. Shooting out from the perimeter of Old Sol are spears of light; pink, gold, red, yellow and crimson all fill the sky as the sun hurries to the horizon. The clouds look like the shields of a victorious army, then suddenly the sun is gone and lo! the curtain of night is down. The master tailor sews his bejewelled charges to the black canopy of the heavens. On high they cluster—the pendants of the constellation Castor, Pollux, Andromeda all glitter in the velvet darkness, like old oily chips on boiled haddock.

April 20th. What a day! The captain mutinied and took over command of the ship. The crew turned really nasty and not one of them would dance with him that evening. The captain finally won the crew around by promising them that they could all try on his hat.

April 21st. As the twilight encroached the ship a knowing looking Irish traveller said, "Them's nice pigeons." I corrected him, "They're gulls." "Well," he replied, "boys or gulls, them's nice pigeons." I was so enraged at his ignorance, I tied him to the mast and gave him sixty lashes with the cat. He's recovered, but the cat's right off its milk.

One day out from the Yemen Peninsular the heat started to play havoc with some passengers, i.e. at dinner a gentleman's shirt front exploded when he saw a lady in a low-cut evening gown. Mind you, her front looked as if it had exploded earlier with a wider area of devastation. The gentleman in question was Charlie Thud, a tea taster from Ceylon who had graduated from tasting soup in the Hebrides, and water at

Tring. (Did you know that Tring was the inventor of the bicycle bell?) In the tourist lounge two Spanish girls and a Flamenco guitarist gave a very sultry concert of Flamenco dancing and singing. I watched spellbound the pounding insistent beat of Spanish rhythms, the red flashing lips of the Senoritas, the sensuous stamping of their heels. In the end, unable to contain myself, I tore off all my clothes, sprang to the middle of the floor and did the Palais Glide. Who said we British didn't have it in us. (I'm writing this from the ship's prison.)

April 22nd. Invited to cocktails with the Captain. He's a real son of the sea. He first became interested in ships when his mother approached him. "John, your father wants you to build a boat at once," she said. "Where is father?" inquired John. "In the middle of the lake, drowning," was the reply. He told me he had the sea in the blood, and believe me you can see where it gets in.

April 23rd. Tonight was held the "Ship's Gala Fancy Dress Ball." I ate three tons of spaghetti, put on a turban and dark glasses, and went as King Farouk, How proud I was till I stepped into the ballroom. Have you ever seen five hundred King Farouks? The bewildered judges threw the prize in the air and we fought for it. Then it was time for some crazy rag (and bone) time rhythm dancing to the wild melodies of Arthur Lovelace and his Arcadian trio. The night grew hotter. Even the champagne was steaming. In the Paul Jones a stout lady grabbed me. "You made a fool of me tonight, fighting for the prize with all those men," and before I could protest she dragged me off to her cabin. "Now take that silly turban and dark glasses off," she said. I did so. She screamed, "Help, there's a strange man in my cabin." The night steward rushed in. "The man is not my husband," she whimpered. "He's not mine either, mum," said the old steward. Well, with five hundred identical King Farouks on board, I bet there was more than one strange moment during the evening. Anyway I was the only one down at breakfast the next morning.

April 24th. What a beautiful morning it's been out on deck. And it was a beautiful morning on the bridge as well. Even on the fo'c'sle head it was a beautiful morning. Only on the third class tourist class passengers' deck was it a sultry overcast dull morning, but then if you do things on the cheap you must expect these things.

Farewell, Neddy,

write soon,

As ever,

SPIKE.

III

What ho! What hi! What hee! There you are dear Neddy Lad, I have given you a selection of *three* cursory greetings all written from memory with the aid of an ordinary portable plastic dog cardigan. Since my last despatch many strange and wondrous things have befallen me, mysteries that only happen in the incense drugged bazaars of the Orient. I have for instance among my purchases, a 2B Pencil made in Cairo, a genuine Sudanese trilby and several original Mona Lisas and all painted (according to the Signature) by the great artist Kodak.

April 3rd. At 0800 hours we sailed through the two light towers flanking the Victoria Dock, Colombo, as the great shining white bulk of the s.s. *Arcadia* steamed towards the jetty, what a reception, bands played, people cheered, maroons were fired, mind you, it all originated on the ship, ashore there wasn't a soul. True to form the native dockers were on strike for less money. They had orginally struck for more; the bosses immediately agreed, so the dockers immediately struck again for less. . . . There had been rioting in the streets, which were patrolled by specially armed police and especially disarmed civilians. There is a saying in the East . . . I can't think of it just now. However, it seemed dangerous to roam abroad in the bazaars, so we made our way on Elephant back to Mount Lavania, site of many heroic incidents in the "Bridge over the Kwai" film. There is now an actual "Bridge over the Kwai" Museum. In one glass case is the head Alec Guinness wore for the film, and by it, nestling on a purple cushion, the bullet wound Jack Hawkins contracted to receive during the shooting of the battle scene. I was told that the battle scene was so well shot, it never recovered and David Lean painted the

60

last part himself. By Midday in Colombo, the heat is so unbearable that the streets are empty save for thousands of Englishmen taking mad dogs for walks. All else is still, the bamboo shop blinds flap idly in the heat, pariah dogs prostrate themselves in the shade of the Bhorum Trees, rickshaw boys deflate their tyres, explode their turbans and snooze on the verandas; Elephants lie cross-ways in the streets to enforce the siesta. Of course they are only life size replicas, real ones would be too big and too expensive, at sundown they are towed out to sea and sunk by Naval Gunfire. There is an old Eastern saying "Thum both atchar adami hai" means You are a good fellow and who knows, they might be. Not long after getting ashore we were invited to have a drink with one of the white residents, an official of the Cortex Oil Co. Inc. He drove us back to his semi-precious bungalow, and we sat on a native sipping iced petrol and nibbling curry cubes. The official was bemoaning the decline of British Prestige in the island. "I can't understand why they don't like us," he said, striking a sleeping native with a stock whip. "I suppose they must have some reason," I suggested, striking the same native with a passing white resident.

It was six o'clock when the meeting broke up, and the *Arcadia* was sailing at midnight. As our taxi hurried back along the Palm fringed golden sanded beaches, the roar of the waves breaking in from the Indian Ocean, conjured up an old English folk poem, There was a young lady of Itchin, who was scratchin' herself in the kitchen, etc. (Traditional).

As the ship's bell rang out the hour of twenty to twelve, the loudspeakers announced all visitors ashore. To make sure no one was left on board the Purser Mr. Harrington went round and with courtesy, only gained by years at sea, threw the remaining visitors over the side, a fitting and noble departure for a great ship. I like promptitude and dislike latecomers. As I write from the wharf, the *Arcadia* is a speck on the horizon. Help!

Regards lad,

Fred Milligan.

E

IV

Hello, merry Seagoon lad! Here I am shivering in seventy-eight degrees of an Australian winter, while you are sweltering in the seventy-five degrees of an English summer. However, I manage to keep warm, lad. I always wear a woollen bathing costume. Of course, this has its disadvantages when riding on a bus. You see, Sydney buses have no swimming pools.

Today I had a friendly letter from home. The postman who delivered it must have had a small piece of jam on his finger (a relic of breakfast days), which had transferred itself to the envelope, and so Ned I had jam for tea! Of course, it didn't go far, but then jam never does—it's perfectly content to stay where it is, but woe betide us all when jam is fitted with an engine! Imagine the headlines: "Old lady knocked down on crossing by marmalade." "We are just good friends," she said. And again, "Squad cars give chase to high powered damson preserve." (If any smart Alec is thinking of cracking the gag about traffic jam, don't! This article is loaded).

But now about dear old hairy Milligoon. Last Sunday I locked my family in the fridge and set off for Avalon Beach, a great majestic sweep of honey gold sand, coral rocks, palm trees, old newspapers, broken bottles, dead horses, forgotten women and Japanese generals who refuse to believe the war is over. Rolling in from the gleaming blue Pacific are the great breakers, and, some of the bodies they've broken. These waves tower up to three hundred and fifty feet high.

(It's true, how *dare* you disbelieve me, why I've just had a ladder gang go up and measure one!).

However, undaunted by their size, I strapped on thirteen life jackets, grasped my surf board, and hurled myself into the kiddies' paddling pool. Despite their protests, I paddled half a length under water. I soon showed them who was master! All except one five year old lad—the gauntlet was down, I closed with him. He threw me on my back, he threw me on my head, he threw me on my knee, on my nose. "Had enough son?" I said, spitting out the last of my milk teeth. He threw me up again. . . .

"Is that your boy you're thrashing?" The voice belonged to a ten foot life saver with two broken noses.

"Of course he is," I lied brilliantly. "Can't you see the resemblance?"

He paused, "How come then he's an aborigine?"

"Oh that? read all about it in next week's *True Confessions.*"

By now the boy had a strangle hold on me, with my legs half way up my back. "Need any help?" asked the two broken noses.

"Yes, if you can hold his hands behind him, I feel I could master him." True to my word I did. Then, exhausted by my running away, I threw myself on to the sand in a victorious heap. Warmed by the sun, and dissipated by a thousand nights of debauchery, I soon fell into a deep sleep.

I was awakened by an earth-quaking roar, and a blast of hot breath that removed both my eyebrows, leaving behind two carbonised tufts. I opened my eyes. (The man who usually opened them was away on another job). Slobbering over me was a lion masquerading as a dog. In his jaws he held half a tree. Seeing me stir he barked, dropped the half tree on to my chest, which drove me three feet deep into the sand. "Shoo, get orf," I shouted from my shallow grave. At this his whole demeanour changed. He snarled, baring a set of yellow fangs that revealed traces of a recently eaten man. "Nice kind doggy," I whined, crawling towards the nearest tree (one hundred and twenty miles away). In one bound, the monster

63

was astride my escape route. Grabbing my ankle in his jaw, he gently crunched the bone and dragged me towards the boiling ocean. His meaning was clear—"Throw the stick or drown." My best plan was to throw the wood and then run for the trees and/or South America. With all the power of my thin arms, I started to swing the great log round and round what, Harry, you laughingly call my head. Faster and faster whirled, then, with one superhuman effort, I hurled it towards the sea. It fell on my foot. Clutching the flattened member, I hopped up and down in agony, accompanied by the monster who was snapping at my rear. What a heroic picture we must have made. Man, dog and clutched foot, all leaping in perfect harmony. But hope drew nigh; from a house a mile away, a pyjama-clad figure on a tricycle hurried towards me. He stopped, and from a safe distance shouted "I say, could you two make less noise, I'm trying to get some sleep."

"So am I," I snarled.

"Yes, but I'm on nights."

"And I'm on nights too." (Actually I was on days, and this was one of them). With his departure, I lost touch with the human race. There was just me, the monster, and half a tree, but the cunning of the human mind is a great weapon, I'd tire the creature out at his own game, ha ha! By midnight I had thrown the log into the sea some eighty-nine thousand times. (It's true, how dare you disbelieve me. I had a ladder gang keep tally of every throw).

I had lost so much weight my trunks wouldn't stay up. With courage born of cowardice, I started to run away. The beast was on me. "Get orf, shoo," I said, and, as an afterthought, *"Help!"* A policeman bounded on to the scene, flashed his torch. "Hello, what's this, trousers round yer ankles?"

I explained in a half gibberish what it was all about.

"Oh," he said, "well in any case you know that dogs aren't allowed on the beach."

"It's not mine."

64

"Oh no? I've been watching you throw sticks for it all day."

"But I. . . ."

Drop me a line, Neddy, c/o Avalon Beach Jail.

Love from

SPIKE.

V

Hello Steaming Harry lad,

Well, now to the dull part; there is, somewhere in the steaming bush of Australia, a waterside town called Woy Woy (Woy it is called Woy Woy oy'll never know). It was founded 2,000 years ago by the lyric Roman poet Terence, but gained no favour until Australians landed there in 1787 with Captain Fred Cook, the then leading agent for Cook's Tours. These were steadily gaining favour with rich convicts, who took the waters of Woy Woy in preference to the penal settlement that charged them ten bob a night for bed, breakfast and hanging.

Nowadays, the old prison has been turned into a first-class hotel with a service that any Michelin guide would be only too pleased to condemn. Built of local stone, it also has a local floor and a local ceiling; buses pass the door and aeroplanes pass the roof. It was to this hotel I was sent on a recommendation. "Go there, son, the fishing is wonderful," said the A.B.C. manager, pocketing the last of my bribes for the radio series.

From Sydney Central, I caught a steam vehicle, on whose sides could faintly be seen the legend—James Watt. For two hours it dragged the carriages through breathtaking scenery, asphyxiating tunnels, and a structure that I swear was a replica of the original Tay Bridge. Before crossing we were all handed a life-belt and a pamphlet on "How to resuscitate the apparently drowned, and how to drown the apparently resuscitated." (Try singing the next bit; it relieves the boredom and helps colonic irrigation). I arrived at Woy Woy soot-black, clutching a banjo, but unharmed save for a skirmish with a dishonest inspector, who forced me to buy a ticket and a length of cheap suiting.

Next morning, with the sun streaming through the holes in my underpants, I left the hotel, and, armed with string, straw hat, a hook, a photo of Isaac Walton and the plans of a fish, made my way to the waterside. As I walked on to the old creaking wood jetty, the warm green waters spread out before me, still and calm, broken only by an occasional fish mouthing an "O" at the surface. All was peace—save for the roar of bulldozers starting work on the Australian end of the Cromwell road extension, and the crash of the mighty bauxite factory that discharges all its nuclear waste into the quiet green waters.

Realizing I was not alone, I donned my trousers. On the end of the jetty sat a gnarled fisherman whose yellow float bobbed hypnotically on the sunlit water. (It's all lies about the bauxite factory and the bulldozers; I put it in to give the article bulk.)

At my approach the fiisherman looked up. He had the finest broken nose I'd ever seen : no matter which way he looked he always appeared to be in profile (O.K. stop singing now). I started the conversation with a typical fisherman's remark, "Had any luck today?" "Yeah, my wife broke her leg." I baited my hook and keeping my eye glued to the instruction book, whirled the line around my head and let go. . . . Splash ! "That your hat floating on the water?" he asked, with a leer on his face. "Yes, must have caught the hook in it." By cutting the brim away I managed to remove the hook, and thus, wearing a wet mutilated hat I continued fishing.

"What bait you using?" he asked.

"Sausages."

"You won't catch anything with them."

"Well, they caught me, I paid a quid for them."

"Here, let me fix you a bait." He threaded a prawn on my hook and ate the sausages.

67

That afternoon wore on, the novelty wore off, and then I felt a nibble on the bait! I pulled up the prawn—thank heaven, it was still safe! To make sure no other fish got it I threw rocks into the water. By keeping up this vigilance till dusk, I preserved the prawn intact. By now my broken-nosed neighbour had caught some 20 black fish. Before he departed he said. "I ain't never seen you around here before."

"No," I said, "I'm from London, I came over to write some comedy shows for radio."

Slowly, very slowly, he said : "Which comedy show?"

"The Goon Show," I said proudly. . . .

It was dark when I regained consciousness, and a policeman stood over me with a torch.

"What happened?" he inquired, picking up the loose teeth that lay around me.

"I was struck down constable, struck down in my prime by a man who forced me to admit I wrote the Goon Show."

The policeman shone his torch closer. "You Spike Milligan?" he said softly.

"I am. . . ."

It was sunrise when I recovered consciousness again. I could hear the sound of shovels at work. I sat up.

"Blast," said one of the shovellers, "He's come to." And he started to fill the hole in.

"Don't worry son, you're safe now." It was my father; he uncrossed my arms and started to rub brandy into my knees, sipping every measure to make sure it wasn't poisoned. Mother held up my fishing rod, "Look, he's caught a prawn," she said.

"That's my boy," said father, staring up the neck of the empty bottle.

I made a hurried calculation. . . . There were only seventy-two shopping days to Christmas!

Farewell Neddy,

Your Pal,

FRED MILLIGAN.

Politics
and Other Nonsense

Come On In, The Fall-out is Lovely

or—they're walking backwards to Aldermaston

Aldermaston Marchers hear this and tremble in the foundations of your sodden Left-Wing shoes. At this very moment, if not sooner, the Milligan inter-party, espionage, phone-tapping, radio-hitting counter-espionage movement has gleaned certain information which should be imparted to you who will shortly march forth (or is it April tenth?) for the cause.

Last night I gained access to Downing Street by merely not causing a disturbance, appearing to have no desire to live, looking utterly indifferent to South Africa's death roll, and executing several Non-U turns in a U-turn street. Discreetly I crawled on to the pavement outside Number Ten.

"Looking for something?" said a policeman.

"Yes," I said, "A new Government."

"You won't find it here, sir, this is the old."

I stood up.

"Who did you vote for?" I said. "Oh, I don't vote," he said. "I'm one of the don't knows."

"I thought I recognized the uniform," I said.

"What are you hinferring, madam?" (He had bad eyesight as well.)

"I am suggesting that there are far too many don't knows. One day the don't knows will get in and then what will happen?"

"I don't know," he said. "Now move along," and he pointed further down.

This, dear reader, was all only a cover-up while I made my way to the International Russian-controlled phone-tapping post at Number Seven. I was welcomed at this door by a Russian girl athlete who put me into a cubicle.

"Just listen in on that," she said pointing to a pair of headphones. "It's ten roubles for three minutes. If Mac's on form you should get some pretty good copy."

At last I'd found it, the Gossip Writer's Nirvana where Tanfield and Hickey exchange notes, here in this simple gutter in Downing Street.

The following is the text of a telephone conversation between the P.M. and Selwyn Lloyd:

Mac: Selwyn?

S. Lloyd: Speaking. What are you doing up so early?

Mac: I'm worried, do you hear me? Worried!

S. Lloyd: Is that Profit Tax hurting the book trade? Say the word and I'll take it——

Mac: No, no, no! Haven't you heard? They're marching again this Easter.

S. Lloyd: Not the Aldermaston lot?

Mac: Yes. The first time—well, we all took it as a joke. Last year there were ten thousand of 'em and to make it even more infuriating they were all orderly. Police were powerless.

S. Lloyd: You think that this year——

Mac: Bigger than ever.

S. Lloyd: Say the word and I'll put a tax on marching——

Mac: No, no, no, Selwyn, no. I've already been planning an alternative march. I've been training 'em for the last three months.

S. Lloyd: How? When? Where? Who? What? Which?

Mac: Steady, Selwyn, don't excite yourself. Remember

74

you're a bachelor. You remember the John O' Groats to Lands End March?

S. Lloyd: Yes, I saw it on the telly.

Mac: What may have appeared a simple publicity stunt by Bill Butlin was in fact a heavily disguised training walk by the Young Conservatives.

S. Lloyd: Floreat Macmillan. . . .

Mac: Ta. At this very moment ten thousand true blue Young Tories are encamped in the Vale of Healthy Hampstead disguised as out of season fair-ground attendants.

S. Lloyd: Master!

Mac: Ta. I, Harold Macmillan, nee Prime Minister, nee Son of Eden, hope to turn the tide by marching in the exact opposite direction! I will march all the way by Rolls Royce.

S. Lloyd: That should put their shares up.

Mac: Following me will be the "Atom Bombs for Peace" group with the banner—*Strontium 90 is Good For You; Get Some Today.* Small miniature flower-clad A-bombs will be exploded *en route* to give festive gaiety to the occasion, and from time to time young Tory back-benchers will jump into the centre of simulated mushroom clouds with cries of— "Look, it doesn't hurt at all!" and/or "Come on in, the fall-out is lovely!"

S. Lloyd: Is that safe?

Mac: I'm not sure. Anyhow, we can afford a few Tories, the woods are full of 'em, eh? Ha ha!

S. Lloyd: We must not take the opposition too lightly though, Mac. There's people among them who think above the waist—even higher.

Mac: Yes, blast 'em!

S. Lloyd: Say the word, Mac, and I'll put a tax on all J. B. Priestleys.

75

Mac: No, no, no. You've done enough for England—to get lung cancer now costs tuppence more—well done Selwyn!

At this point the great British G.P.O. system working true to its ecstatic form collapsed . . . however, we had heard enough, so, friends, don't forget to march in the opposite direction to the you-know-whos!

F

My Court Martial

The following is just a thought. I recall the incident from my old Army days. In 1917 the British invented the military tank. Under conditions of great secrecy an attack on the German lines was prepared at Cambrai.

The day before the attack, however, to the amazement of all, the Germans attacked the British with tanks. Immediately a member of the House of Commons demanded an inquiry into our security methods.

First day of the inquiry before the Lords Blimley, Grumper, and Chatsshaw-Blurtington.

Mr. Smith, K.C.: Lord Spike, you are a General in the British Army?

Lord Spike: Ermm. Yes.

Smith, K.C.: Your salary is £3,000 a year?

Lord Spike: Errrmm. Yes.

Smith, K.C.: You consider that a living wage?

Lord Spike: Errmm. Well, errr——

Smith: You are living. . . ?

Lord Spike: Yes.

Smith: Then you must be getting a living wage.

(Laughter)

Smith: Lord Spike, you knew of the promised British tank attack three days before it happened?

Spike: Yes. I had been told by the Minister for War.

Smith: You told no one else?

Spike: No.

Smith: Lord Spike, what I am to reveal to the court may displease you, but reveal it I must. I have here before me a receipt addressed to you from the German Army. It says: "For services rendered, 10,000 Deutschesmarks."

Spike: I fail to see why the revelation should displease me.

Smith: For what reason do you receive these payments from the German Army?

Spike: I happen to be a Director : have been for several years.

Smith: I see; in fact you have shares in the German Army.

Spike: Yes.

Smith: Lord Spike, is not your loyalty divided between the German and British cause?

Spike: Of course not; I serve each office faithfully.

Smith: Let me amplify your position. Supposing, only supposing, the German Army are building up for an attack on the British. What is your immediate reaction.

Spike: As a director of the German Army it is my duty to keep secret from the British their intention.

Smith: But you are General of the British Army. In the light of your knowledge, should you not make defensive preparations?

Spike: Of course not. It would ill become my position as a shareholder in the German Army. No sir. When the Germans attacked, and only when, would I react.

Smith: You actually mean you are almost Schitzoid in that respect?

Spike: Putting it clinically, er—yes.

Smith: Regarding the tank attack, as the British had only just invented the tank, was it not a great coincidence that the Germans invented it three days before?

Spike: It certainly did surprise me—as a British General, that is. Of course, as a shareholder in the German Army I knew all the time.

Smith: Can you explain why three days prior to the British tank attack a telegram was delivered to the German High Command reading : "Build tanks"?

Spike: It was just coincidence.

Smith: As the result of the successful German tank attack did not the shares you hold in the German Army increase in value?

Spike: Ermmm. Yes.
Smith: That is all, Lord Spike.
From here on I let the reader take over.

Crossword for Idiots

Across

   1. The indefinite article.

Down

   1. First letter of alphabet.

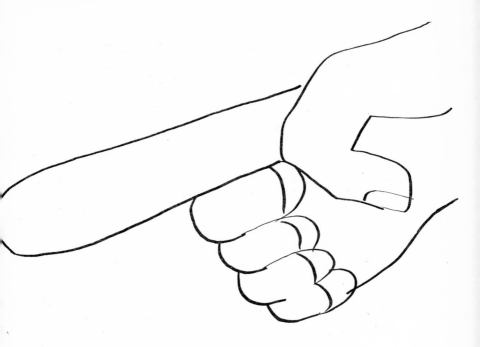

ARREST THAT MAN. !

Lance-Corporal Spike Milligan Joins the Ministry of Defence

By paying a search fee of five shillings, and suffering the customary insults of civil servants, I was allowed to see the marriage registers of Somerset House.

After three hours among the M's, I discovered what I had hoped, there was a marriage of my great-great-grandfather, Timothy Brian Boin Milligan to Miss Jill *Macmillan*.

I was in! Related to the P.M.! For several hours, wearing a hand-made Clan Macmillan centrally-heated kilt, I stood in a queue of Macmillans outside Number Ten.

Finally, about dividend time, I was shown in to the great man.

"Do sit down," he said, indicating the floor. "Be with you in a jiff," he said, and proceeded to put on several Eton, two Harrow and three Lords Taveners' ties. "Got to keep in with 'em," he yawned, "it's the only way these days." A G.P.O. Democratic monopoly phone rang.

"Hello, Prime Minister of England here. . . . No no, not yet, we'll wait for the Ford hoo ha to die down first before the next one. Bye Henry, oh, Henry? . . . tell them to lay off any take-over bids of publishing firms eh? There's a good boy. Bye now.

He turned to me, "So, you're one-tenth Macmillan?"

"Yes I am, sir."

"We can still be friends, eh? ha, ha, suppose you want a job?"

I nodded. "Look, we're a bit short of speeches for the Minister of Defence, he's been slipping lately, I mean, making statements that have no double entendre. If you can write one that well, one that well, er well you know, one that er. . . ."

"I *think* I know *exactly* what you mean sir."

"Good boy, you've got the right idea . . . now, do you own *a* pencil?"

"Outright."

"Splendid, here's a White Paper, fill it in."

He shook me by the hand, gave me a travel voucher and a Macmillan's Christmas Catalogue of "Suitable Book Presents for Members of All Parties. Free postage to our clients in USSR."

At dawn, after the Christmas recess, Mr. Harold Watkinson, Minister of Defence, read from my typewritten paper.

Hansard Report of Defence Speech—1961

Mr. Speaker, Honorable Members . . . (here there were cries of p——off, from Opposition Back Benchers). This morning, I have pleasure in giving the Government's estimate for next year's Defence Budget 1961-62. Eight hundred and forty-five million, two hundred and sixty-three hundred thousand, three hundred and forty-two pounds, eight shillings and eightpence three farthings. Postage, four and a penny.

Extras and taxi fares—nine million, three hundred and forty-nine thousand, six hundred and spon. This puts our Defence Budget up by four hundred million on last year. (Applause from Tory benches. At this stage Mr. Crapington Plitt, Liberal M.P. for a tree in Berkshire, intervened.)

Mr. Crapington Plitt: Does this mean we are in fact safer?

Min. of Defence: Of course, we are obviously four million pounds safer, less super tax of course.

Mr. Crapington Plitt: Do the Russians know this?

Min. of Defence: No . . . no . . . but we will be sending them our military bank statement, and, *that* ought to give them food for thought. Ha, ha.

(Light applause, tea, cakes, and scratching from Tory benches break out.)

Mr. Feet, M.P.: What plans are being made for our Forces at Christmas?

Min. of Defence: All is in hand, the time of goodwill will be observed, with its message of Christmas hope for mankind.

Mr. Feet: What form will this take?

Min. of Defence: All inter-continental ballistic missiles will be festooned with fairy lights, and nuclear war heads hung with seasonal holly.

Mr. Squtts (M.P. for a lunatic asylum in Alleppo): But these missiles you speak of, they're not British... !

Min. of Defence: Ah no! but . . . *but!* . . . their presence here puts Britain in a position of power, this great deterrent that has given us peace on earth and goodwill to all men for so long, is now on British soil . . . I. . . .

(Cries of "American bum," and a cry of "Let's have a little more libel" from Strangers' Gallery. A man called Randolph is asked to leave.)

Min. of Defence: I admit that these bases have been built by Americans, manned by Americans, and that Americans alone have the power to decide if and when the missiles are fired, but, nevertheless and as much as thereto, the men who sweep the missiles' platforms and stand guard in the pouring rain are *British!*

(Ecstatic applause, from the Tory benches, singing of National Anthem breaks out. Speaker restores order by distributing non-voting G.M.C. shares.)

Mr. Feet (Labour): In the event of an H-bomb dropping on Aldershot, what would be the role of our troops?

Min. of Defence: The prime job of our Army is to defend England, but, should an H-bomb fall on Aldershot, the troops would be transported to safety, to say Scotland, and stand ready to defend England.

Mr. Mac Nutts (Labour): Supposin' that they drop an H-bomb on Scotland . . . Ireland, Wales and, well, the lot?

Min. of Defence: The Army would be flown to the safety of Canada, and stand ready to defend England from there.

Mr. Feet: Are you saying that it is possible for H-bombs to destroy England?

Min. of Defence: Never! There'll always be an England.

Mr. Feet: Never mind England—what about the English people?

Min. of Defence: Oh *them*?

(Here the Labour Backbenchers took to song with—"There'll always be a Radio-active England." Fighting, Foot and Mouth and Kingsley Martin broke out, etc., etc.)

HANSARD.

Dated—December, 1961.

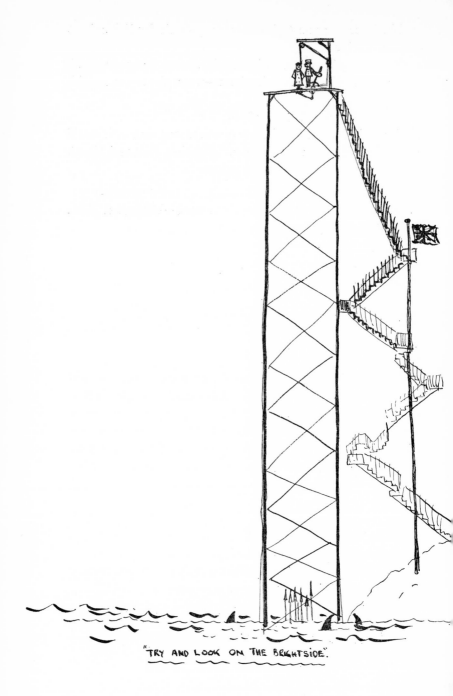

"TRY AND LOOK ON THE BRIGHTSIDE".

How to Make a Foon

For those who are fortunate enough to be given a Foon next Christmas, it will be necessary to explain the functions of it. The Foon is packed in zinc wrapping and contained in a large wooden crate marked *(dn ʎɒɯ sıɥ⊥)* (I bet you turned the page upside down. I did.) Now, the Foon can give years of pleasure to those who know how to assemble and use it. There is, however, the slight danger of Strontium 90, which is ever present in the central chamber of the Foon. However, we won't worry about that until later.

First remove the lid of the crate with the crowbar you will find inside. Insert the chisel end of the bar under the corners and prise open upwards; if you have to prise downwards this means the crate is upside down *(sıɥʇ ǝʞıⱢ)*. Once open, the rest is simple. Oh yes, as I said previously, there is a minute possibility of the Strontium 90 radiating from the Foon, so my advice to the lucky owner is to buy an ordinary geiger counter, such as you might find in any average American's home. These can be bought from the Surplus Army Stores, or direct from the Surplus Army itself : write to them, enclosing a three-guinea postal order. Allowing for railway strikes, go slows, and general national decadence, your geiger counter should arrive within a month—if it is marked "Urgent, Life or Death."

Connect the geiger to a three-volt AC/DC battery; hold the counter over the corner of the Foon container and move it horizontally backwards and forwards listening, ever listening for the staccato clicks that will warn you of Strontium 90! . . . One little point, in case, just in case, the geiger counter is fautly, it would be a wise added precaution to hire or buy an official Harwell lead lined anti-gamma-ray suit . . . these are not in the shops yet. But you can get one from any Russian Embassy, provided you sign a newspaper article headed "How the Russians saved me from Capitalist Gamma Radiation in My *Own* Country." Be sure the suit fits well around the wrists, ankles and neck. If it doesn't it doesn't matter. I know this must all be disheartening, but it is well worth it when you consider the pleasure yet to come from your Christmas Foon.

By now, we should be dressed in our anti-gamma suit, and holding our geiger counter pass it slowly over the top . . . no clicks? Then all is well! . . . but, alas! it is almost certain that there will be a high degree of clicking as the Christmas Foon is always radio-active. So you see, my advice on anti-gamma suits was very wise.

As the Foon is proving highly dangerous, it obviously can't be kept in the house, especially if you have a family. What then? "How can I enjoy the pleasure of my Foon," you say: it is simple—the Ministry of Atomic Research have published a jolly little handbook on how to house dangerous fissionable materials in your own back garden (oh goody!) Dig a hole twenty-six feet square, and thirty-two feet deep; line the inside with concrete to a thickness of no less than three feet. If you haven't any concrete, lead plate will do. (Make sure that there are no perforations of any kind in the linings of your socks.)

The staircase down to the pit should have a shower (warm and cold) for all people entering or leaving the Foon chamber . . . (I bet you can't wait to get it installed).

Weather permitting, the Foon housing chamber should be ready by early February, and February should be ready by early March. Install a few chairs and tables, a bedside light, and one or two nude women—make the place homely. . . .

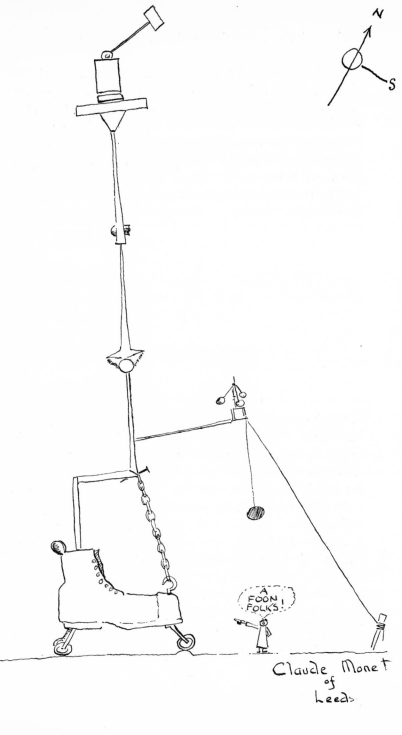

Claude Monet
of
Leeds

And now! the installation of the Foon! (Here we all stand and shout "Huzza.")

For those who may not have seen one before, I include this diagram. If you hold this page up to the light you will be able to see the outline of the internal structure. Now bolt Section A to B, L, D and X : insert nozzle at pricked pinmark Spon : lift krudgeon lever on to Plinn bolt (see diagram 3), and thrust multi-purpose stick into multi-purpose hole, and paint red where red is not visible. Thrust head into bracket, and fix neck on to lead plate with foot-operated mallet one inch from back of skull. *Warning:* keep feet in line with seams of trousers.

Foon; internal structure. Hold to light.

Press plunger A, and push button marked B-U-T-T-O-N. The owner of the Foon is now in complete control and in mortal danger! The hammer should descend on the back of the owner's skull with sickening rapidity. Unpack section D in the base locker marked First Aid : swallow contents immediately, and unpack carton marked Phone. Dial nine, nine, nine, and in that order. By now the Foon should have its owner in a vice-like death grip, and be creating great welts on the back of his head. However, too much of a good thing is dangerous, so those who are standing around enjoying the spectacle should try and extricate the lucky screaming owner as soon as he's had enough, lay him face downwards on his back, and bring his knees up under his chin—starting at the bottom and working up.

92

Within a matter of days the 999 call should have been answered, and an ambulance with a piece of holly on the bonnet should have arrived. As the Foon owner drives away for the hospital, give a merry wave and say, "Next year I too must get a Foon."

The Dread Anti-Breakfast-In-Bed League

Dear Hotel Traveller,

This letter is to forewarn you all of a secret society of Hotel Employees, all pursuing an insidious course, bent on casting a crepuscous gloom on humble partakers of early morning breakfast. Let me recount the horror I have suffered at the hands of those who run what is laughingly called "The Greatest Hotel in the Midlands."

Last winter, my doctor had told me I was suffering from a lack of money. Clutching a National Health free week-end hotel voucher, I caught the night train to the Midlands. It is a sad thought, dear reader, that, no matter how modern a hotel, no matter how sublime the architecture, no matter how excellent the interior comfort, all is sublimated when you come face to face with that itinerant species, the grey-minded hotel staff.

The king of all hotels is the Porter; uppermost in his tiny subconscious mind is the legend "Britons never never never shall be Slaves." Any favour they do, even in the course of their duty, is done with the air of forced sufferance and condescension, by their attitude, they reduce the client to the level of a grovelling minion, where even the paying of the bill is looked upon as disgusting.

The softening-up process starts at Lunch, where a blue-chinned cretin disguised as the head waiter, hands you the Menu. Before you can cast an eye on it, he whips it away and, loking disdainfully past you, says in a loud semi-continental disembodied voice, *"The Aylesbury duck is very good."*

If you are arrogant enough to refuse, he spits, turns his

back, and leaves you in the hands of some spotty Greek Herbert, whose attitude can only be described as EOKA. The intention is to raise your ire to such a pitch that, by the time you do get what you ordered, you have no stomach for it.

The Somnelier is a cut above this, but he in turn hides from any oenophillic diner. Tracker dogs are sent, and finally towards the end, he arrives in time to serve you chilled Claret and warm Riesling with your coffee. Should you linger a few wayward moments after your brandy, the staff hover round the table wearing pyjamas and waving the bill on a reeking garlic-ridden pole.

This all happened to me dear reader. The same night, I closed with the Night Porter. He grudgingly entered my order for breakfast in bed on the sodden pages of a Note Book.

"Six Forty be orl rite for yern," he said, looking past me.

I put on a friendly voice. "Well, isn't that a bit early?"

"Not fer me. I'll be up till then."

"Ha, ha, but tomorrow's Sunday, I'd like to have it about 8.30."

With lizard-heavy lids he looked at me, while he spat on his finger and erased the figures six-thirty. . . . He sucked the air in through his teeth.

"Orl rite then . . . eight-thirty."

"Could I have a Sunday Paper as well?"

". . . we'll see."

As I walked towards the lift I thought I heard him mutter a four-letter relative of the word in Lady C.

I lapsed into sleeping consciousness, dreaming of that aromatic breakfast in bed. There came a strange hammering at the door and a strangulated voice which sounded as if the owner was wearing an ill-fitting truss. I looked at the watch : five-forty. "What is it," I said angrily.

A voice grunted a groaning reply.

"It's yourn breakfast. . . ."

"It can't be, I ordered it for eight-thirty. . . ."

95

"It's nuffink ter do wiv me, mate. I was told five-forty."

There followed a further clattering, groaning and half-hearted door knob rattling. Exasperated, I bid him enter.

"I carn't," came the groaning reply. "I ain't gort the key...."

"What about the pass key?"

"Oh, I don't know nuffink 'bout that, mate. I'm noo 'ere."

This was the war of nerves method of the "Anti-Breakfast-in-Bed League." Their task was to see, that no matter what you had to be got from your bed; once they'd done that, their moral victory had been asserted. My task was to get from my bed, open the door, and get back into bed before he saw me, otherwise, the breakfast tray would be thrust into my hand, and the Spectre de la Breakfast would be gone, rubbing his hands and sending another successful report to "The League." In one tigerish bound I opened the door, and just managed to dive under the blankets as he rushed into the room, breathing heavily; he could see I had foiled his master move. For three minutes he stood silently in the doorway waiting for my nerve to crack.

"Come in, shut the door, and put the breakfast down," I said in a commanding voice. He pushed the door with his foot, leaving it open, for passing morning maids to giggle at my ruffled dawn face. It was part of the plan. For several minutes he wandered aimlessly round the room, bumping into furniture. "It's meeyes," he moaned. To frighten me, he stumbled several times. Finally he put it down on a suit case, on the far side of the room. "Anything else," he says making for the out. "Yes, I'd like that breakfast tray by my bed." He faltered, clumsily, he made heavy weather of pulling the suit case across the room, then cunningly, when almost within reaching distance he played his trump card. "Oh," he groaned, with a look of agony on his face. "Me back's gorn, me back, I'll send another bloke up," he said and ran laughing from the room.

The smell of the breakfast pervaded the room, the temptation was too great; cautiously I stepped from my bed, hastened across the room . . . there was a cough behind me, I turned, he had returned.

"Oh," he grinned, "I see you've got out of bed."

I'd lost, the League had chalked up another victim.

Fairy Tales

A COUPLE OF FAIRY TALES WHICH MY CHILDREN HAVE ENJOYED
(at pistol point)

A Witch's Tale

Once upon a time there was a little boy and girl, the girl was called Mary and the little boy was called Tommy. One day, as they were on their way home, they saw an *old* woman with a *long* black cloak and *long* pointed ginger boots and a white face with purple eyes and a long pointed nose.

She said, "Hello little children, won't you buy one of my nice packets of bubble soap?"

And they said, "No, we haven't any money."

She said, "Never mind little children : have one for nothing," and she held out a large packet of yellow powder. "Put it in your bath," she said, "It will make the whole bath full of lovely yellow bubbles."

So, the children took this yellow powder, and that night they got into their bath and they emptied *all* the yellow powder in. All of a sudden a terrible thing happened! They felt themselves getting *smaller* and *smaller* and smaller! They got *so* small that when their mummy came to empty the bath, she couldn't see them. She pulled the plug out and the children went right down the drain, down and down, down *right* under the ground! It was dark *very* dark. They were shouting "Help help! help!" but their voices were *so* tiny no one could hear them. Then they saw a little speck of light in the distance, and they knew they were coming near the end of the drain. There was a terrible sound of roaring water and then *pop*! and out they popped.

They found themselves in a big wide stream in the country-side. They grabbed hold of a brown leaf that was floating by and pulled themselves on. (Now what do you think made the children get so small? The powder? Yes, it was a *magic* yellow powder.)

Suddenly, a great shadow fell across the children and a long thin hand reached out towards them. They heard a terrible cackling sound. "He, he, he, he, he, he, he," and they saw a great white face and they saw she had long pointed ginger boots—it was the old woman who gave them the yellow powder. What was she? She was a witch. "He, he, he, he, he," she said, "Got you!" and popped them into a glass pickle jar. She jumped on a broomstick and *flew* up into the sky. Up and up and up she went until she came to a great black cloud full of thunder. She flew round and round the cloud and screamed a magic word, "Yim-bon balla boo-yim-bon balla boo." And a great door in the side of the cloud opened. In she flew, for inside the cloud was a great red witch's palace, all made of glass and animal bones. She took them into a great room, full of frogs.

She put them on a table and the little boy said, "What are you going to do with us?"

She said, "I'm going to turn you into a pair of black Giant-boots," and she made a magic pass and said some secret words, "Tip-a-tip a Par-par Ti-po-tee-O-Yiggerely-Jiggerely—one two three!"

Fhooshhhhh! The children disappeared in a cloud of orange and mauve smoke and in their place was a pair of black Giant-boots. The poor children had been changed into boots!

Just then, there was a great knocking on the door, Bom-Bom-Bom! The Witch said, "Who is there?" ... And a great voice said, "It's Giant Jim ... have you got my black Giant-boots ready...?"

"Yes, I have, he, he, he," she said.

"Are they made of children?" he said.

102

The Witch!

"Yes they are," said the witch.

"*Good,*" he said, "I like my boots to be made of children," and he sat down and tried them on. "Oh they fit me fine, how much?"

She said, "I don't want money. I want you to catch me a Kangaroo, because I want to have a Kangaroo tail stew!"

The Giant was puzzled. He said, "Er what's a Kangaroo?" (What is a Kangaroo children? What does a Kangaroo do —hops?).

The Witch said, "Go to Australia, there're *plenty* of Kangaroos there."

(Are there Kangaroos in Australia? No, yes). So that's where the Giant Jim went. He was so tall he only had to take three paces to get from England all the way to Australia, and there he was, Giant Jim in the middle of the Australian Desert.

Now this Giant was very stupid. He couldn't remember his name. He said, "Oh my name is—er—Giant Tom? Er— dat's right, my name's Giant Tom, isn't it? Oh Giant Jim? Oh Taarrr, my name is Giant ... er Jim. I've come to Australia to look for a er . . . er . . . Elephant, no no no not an Elephant . . . ah a Kangaroo. . . dat's it." So he kept an eye open for a Kangaroo.

Soon along came a Kangaroo. And his name was Fred Fertangggg. His name was Fred Fertanggg. He was called that because when he hopped he went Fertang! Fertang! Fertang!

The Giant saw him and grabbed him. "Got him! I've caught a Kangaroo. Hooray!"

Now, you remember that little Mary and Tom were the Giant's boots? So Mary said, "Let's pinch his feet so he has to take us off," so the *squeezed* and *squeezed* until the boots hurt his feet so much he shouted. "Oh my feet, oh my poor old tootsies. Oh these boots are too small. I'll take 'em off." He was so angry he went back to the Witch's palace in the clouds and he said, "I want a new pair of boots, these are too small. Look at my poor tootsies, they're going doing-doing."

104

She said, "Have you got the Kangaroo yet?"

He said, "I'm not giving it to you until you make these boots bigger."

She said, "Oh dear it means I'll have to change the boots back into children, then I'll have to make the children bigger and then I'll turn them into bigger boots." She took the boots into her room and she threw a magic red and green powder at them. And, the boots turned back into Mary and Tommy again. "Now," she said, "Now where's that orange powder. . . ." And, as she turned her back to get it, the children ran out of the room and slammed the door.

Outside, the Giant said, "Oh! who are you?"

They said, "The Witch sent us out to look after your Kangaroo while you go and get your new boots."

"Oh," he said, "O.K.! hold him," and he gave them Fred Fertangggg.

As soon as he'd gone, the children jumped into the Kangaroo's pocket and said, "Hop it . . . or we'll all be killed." Off hopped Fred Fertang, Fertang! Fertang! Fertang!

He kept hopping till they were far away in a big forest full of great brown trees that reached up almost to the sky.

Inside it was all dark, and Tommy said to Mary, "We'll be safe here from the Witch and the Giant; it's too dark for them to see us."

But right behind them they heard the crashing sound of the Giant. He was pulling all the trees up. And up above they could hear the Witch flying on her broomstick saying, "After them, after them, ha, ha, ha, ha."

The Giant was getting very close . . . closer . . . closer! But just then Fred Fertang saw a little tiny hole in a tree. Fertang hopped inside. Inside the tree was a little tiny room with a tiny little yellow light in the middle. At a little table sat a little goblin with a red hat, green trousers, pink jacket and purple and white boots.

"Who are you?" said the children.

105

The Giant.

"My name is Oggley Poogley, I'm the keeper of the Gentle Dragon."

"Oh please help us Oggley Poogley. There's a Giant called Jim after us; he's pulling up all the trees."

"Pulling up all the trees," said Oggley Poogley looking very angry and waggling his eyebrows. "He mustn't do that, these trees are Dragon's food. I'll soon stop him." And he went outside, looked up at the Giant and said, "Hey you, stop pulling up those trees."

The Giant said, "No I won't. You want to fight?"

The goblin said, "No, I'm too small, but I'll get you a fight." And he took a little blue whistle and he blew it. Then there was a terrible noise from inside the forest. A great crashing, and through the trees came the Goblin's Dragon. He was as tall as ten houses, and covered in thick red skin with purple stripes; he had a mouth full of sharp teeth like knives. When the Giant saw him, he was frightened; he let out a yell, "Help, help," and he started to run away. The Dragon chased him and breathed a great stream of flames at him and he set the Giant's trousers on fire. "Oh help," he shouted, and all his trousers were burnt at the back and his shirt tail was hanging out.

Then the goblin blew his whistle and the Dragon came back. "Don't be frightened of him," said the goblin. "He won't hurt, he's a *good* Dragon."

"Oh please help us, we want to be big like we were before the Witch turned us into midgets," said the children.

"Oh," said the goblin. "There's only one person who could do that. He's the Great Wizard called Bongg. He lives in an Eagle's nest at the top of a great Silver Palace right up the mighty snow mountains."

"How do we get there," said the children.

"Well," said the goblin, "You'd better jump in Fred Fertang's pocket again and tell him to follow the forest road until he gets to the Milk River. When you arrive there you will see an old Yellow Owl wearing trousers and a school cap: ask him what to do."

Oggley - Poogley

Before they went he gave them a golden pebble. "If ever you want me," he said, "Rub this on your hand."

So, off they went in Fred Fertang's pocket. Fertang! Fertang! Fertang! The sun was going down when they arrived at the Great Milk River. It was all milk, and, all along the banks pussy cats were drinking from it. But there was *no* sign of the owl. "Twit-two whit." They looked up, and *there* he was, in a tree, wearing a shirt and a school cap.

"You looking for me?"

"Yes we are," said the children. Oggley Poogley, the goblin, said you would show us the way across the Milk River to the Great Wizard called Bong!"

"Oh yes," said the owl. "You'll have to go part of the way by Flying Pussy Cat." And he pointed to a great white pussy cat with a propellor on the end of his tail. "Get on my back," said the cat. They all jumped into his fur. "Hold tight," said the cat. The propellor on his tail started to go round and round. Up and up and up he flew, over the Milk River, over the houses, over the trees and the lakes.

Down below they could see trees with chocolate apples growing on them. "Oh! I'd like one of those," said Fred Fertang, the Kangaroo, so, the pussy cat flew *very* low, and, as they went over the trees, they all grabbed a chocolate apple. On and *on* they flew!

Suddenly, the cat's propellor stopped. "Oh, help," he said, "Help, we're falling, something's wrong! My tail's run out of petrol." Down and down they came, faster and *faster* and FASTER. *Crash. . .* ! Luckily, they all fell on to a big hay cart. Wheee dong! wheee dong! wheee donggg! All three landed safely.

"Oo's that in there," said a voice. It was the driver of the hay cart. "Come out of there or I'll poke you with my stick." Pokey, pokey, pokey. They all crawled out.

"What are you doing in there," he said.

"We're looking for the Wizard called Bong," said Tommy.

"Oh, dear," he said, "That's a dangerous journey. I'll take

you as far as I can, so you'd better have a sleep." So they fell off to sleep.

All night long they slept in the cart, and soon it started to snow. "All right, you three get off here," said the cart driver. They all jumped down. "Mind how you go. There're terrible dangers ahead for you all. Good luck!" and off he went.

The children jumped into Fred Fertang's pocket and up the snowy road he hopped. Fertang, Fertang, Fertang. Oh it was cold, all their noses went red. They saw a big sign BEWARE OF THE DANGEROUS WHITE RABBIT.

They thought, "That's funny, how can a rabbit be dangerous?"

"Who said dat?" said a voice from a hole in the ground, and out popped a white rabbit.

"Are you the dangerous white rabbit?" they asked.

"Yes, I'm the dangerous white rabbit," he said.

"Why are you dangerous?" asked the children.

"I eat grass, I'm dangerous to grass. Now, where are you all going?" said the White Rabbit.

"We are going to see the Wizard called Bong."

"Oh, I've always wanted to meet him, can I come too?" said the Rabbit. So into Fred Fertang's pocket he popped.

As they turned a bend in the road, there in the middle was a great Tiger. *Grrr*. He sprang at them, and swallowed them all up, *Gulp*. And there were, Mary, Tommy, Fred Fertang and the White Rabbit, all inside the Tiger's tummy.

It was very dark inside the Tiger's tummy. Only when the Tiger opened his mouth to growl did the light get in. "Don't worry," said the White Rabbit, "I've got some matches and a candle." So he lit a candle. He held the candle up, and all the smoke started to go round the Tiger's tummy and made him feel ill. Oh he felt so sick. All his stripes fell off. The candle started to burn his tummy and he started to cough and cough and cough. Huh *Cough, cough . . . coughhh*. And he coughed so much he coughed out all the children, the Kangaroo and

110

the Rabbit. And while he was still coughing, Tommy rubbed the golden pebble that the goblin gave him and made a wish. There was a rush of wind, and a strange sound, Hoing! A little blue light appeared in the sky. It came rushing down, there was a flash, and a puff of smoke. And there was a Giant Black Man.

"I am the slave of the golden pebble, whatever you ask me to do, I will do."

"Please can you take us to the Palace of the Wizard called Bong?"

"Your wish is my command." He clapped his hands. And there was a flying carpet. "Jump on that carpet and it will take you to his Palace."

On they jumped and up went the carpet, flying through the sky. And the carpet went so fast that the wind nearly blew them off. Faster and faster they went. And there down below, on top of a snowy mountain, they saw a Silver Palace.

"That's the Wizard's Castle," said White Rabbit, and the magic carpet started to go down and down and down. And they got slower and slower. As they were flying over the roof of the Wizard's Castle, they heard a terrible cackling. "He! he! he!" and there flying above them, was the Witch!

"I'll have you now," she said. But the magic carpet flew through the window of the Wizard's Castle and landed on the floor, right by the Wizard's bed. He was fast asleep. When he heard the noise, he woke up.

"Oh dear, dear, dear, what's going on?" he said.

"There's a black Witch after us," said the White Rabbit.

"Oh, we'll soon fix her," said the Wizard called Bong. He picked up a big gun, full of mud, and he fired it at her. And Splosh! It hit her right in the face. Down she came, *Splash*! right in the big lake.

"Now," said the Wizard called Bong, "What's the trouble?"

"Please can you make us like ordinary size children again?"

111

The Wizard.

"Yes," said the Magician. "Now, all stand against that wall and close your eyes." He took a long glass rod with a star on the end, and he tapped the children on the nose. And bong-bong-bong-veroom, they went back to their own size again.

"Now, off you go home," said Bong the Wizard.

They all jumped on to the magic carpet, and up in the sky they went. But, the Witch, she was waiting for them. After she'd fallen in the water, she changed herself into a cloud of smoke. So, when the children saw her, they didn't know it was her.

"Oh, look," said the Rabbit, "There's a smoke cloud following us."

A little bird flew over them, "Be careful of that smoke, it's the Witch," he cried.

So Mary and Tommy got a paper bag, and they waited till the smoke cloud was very near, then they popped it over the smoke and caught it all in the bag.

And they could hear her inside the bag shouting. "Let me out, let me out, let me out!"

But they didn't let her out, and the magic carpet went faster and faster, up, up, up into the clouds, and there they were, flying through clouds back home.

113

When they got home, their Mummy and Daddy were so pleased to see them, and the White Rabbit and Fred Fertang and Tommy and Mary lived happily ever after.

But what happened to the Witch? She's *still* inside the paper bag! He! He! He!

The Gingerbread Boy

Once upon a time there was a baker man and his wife. They lived in a little mill by a stream full of fish and fat frogs. It was all very lovely, *but* the baker and his wife were very, *very* unhappy—do you know why? Well they didn't have any children.

"Oh, I *wish* I had a little boy all of my own."

When the baker saw his wife crying, he said, "Don't cry, wife. I will try and get us a little boy."

So, that night, he went to the bakery and said to himself, "If we can't have a real baby, I'll make one." So—he got a big bag of white flour and he mixed it with water until it was a big ball of dough—it looked like a big snowball—then he took a jar of ginger and mixed it into the dough. All night he worked, and do you know what he was doing? He was making a gingerbread boy. He made the legs, then the arms, the body, and last he made the gingerbread boy's head. Do you know how he made the eyes? How would you make a gingerbread boy's eyes? Well, this is how the baker made them: he got two currants and popped them in, then he made a little heart out of peppermint and put it inside the body.

When it was all ready he put the gingerbread boy into the oven to make him nice and warm. After a little while the miller heard a tiny voice. "Let me out, let me out. It's hot in here!" Do you know who it was saying it? The gingerbread boy! Quickly, the miller took him out of the oven and he saw the gingerbread boy was alive!

"Hello, my boy," said the miller.

"Who are *you*?" said the gingerbread boy.

"I am your daddy." And he picked him up and kissed him.

115

Then little gingerbread boy said, "What is my name?" The miller said, "I don't know yet. I will take you home and ask your mother."

"Oh, let's hurry," said gingerbread boy, and off they ran to the miller's house. When his wife opened the door and she saw gingerbread boy she was so happy she clapped her hands with joy. "At last! At last I have a little boy all of my own. I shall call him 'Gingy' because he is a ginger colour."

Next morning they took Gingy to start school. At first Gingy was very happy in school, but then one day a naughty boy called Tommy bit Gingy on the arm. "Oh!" said poor Gingy and Tommy said, "You taste like a bit of gingerbread," and he bit poor Gingy again.

The poor little gingerbread boy started to run home—oh dear—it started to rain and he started to get all soggy, and when he arrived home he was just a big ball of dough, like he first was.

When his mother saw him she started to cry and cry. "Boo-hoo-hoo, what has happened to my poor boy." And her tears came running down all over gingerbread boy.

"Please don't cry all over me, or I'll fall into little pieces," said Gingy.

"Come here. I'll make you all better again," said the baker, and he squeezed all the rain out of gingerbread boy and made him back into a proper boy again.

That night, when they tucked him into bed, gingerbread boy said, "Mummy, why do I crumple away when it rains?" So mummy had to tell him—he was made of gingerbread, and he was not the same as other girls and boys.

That night little gingerbread boy was very sad. He didn't want to be just made of bread—he wanted to be made of skin.

"I'm going to run away." So he put on his clothes and took three apples and two oranges in a bag and off he tramped into the forest behind the house. It was dark as black, and a big owl said, "Where are *yoo* going *tooo*?"

116

"Please owl, I'm cold and tired and hungry. Can I shelter under your wing?"

"Oh, all right," said the owl.

Underneath the wing it was nice and warm, and gingerbread boy went fast asleep. When he woke up it was morning and the owl said, "I must be off now. I'm going to bed." And away he flew to bed—because owls don't sleep at night, only in the daytime.

Now gingerbread boy was alone again and he walked through the woods till he came to the top of a hill—and there he saw a house. It was a very funny house—it didn't have any windows, only lots and lots of doors. Gingerbread boy knocked at one door, and out came a funny old man wearing a long blue shirt and no trousers.

"What do you want?" he said.

"I'm hungry," said gingerbread boy, "and I'm cold."

The old man took him inside. "I'll soon have you warm. Just get into this nice bath of hot water."

Splash. In jumped gingerbread boy. "Oh, this is lovely," he said, and then a terrible bad thing happened—gingerbread boy started to come to pieces in the hot water. "Help! Help!" he cried, "Get me out!" But it was too late.

The funny old man rolled all the pieces into a big ball of dough and put it on the mantlepiece. Next morning the funny old man went to the market and tried to sell the big piece of gingerbread. No one would buy it, but then along came gingerbread boy's daddy, the baker.

"I need some dough," he said, so he bought it off the old man for a penny.

Now, the baker didn't *know* it was really the gingerbread boy he had bought but, when he got back to the bakery, he saw the little peppermint heart sticking out of the lump of gingerbread.

"Hooray, I've found my gingerbread boy again!" And quickly, quickly he made the gingerbread boy all over again, just like he used to be.

117

"Oh, daddy, daddy," said gingerbread boy. "I'll never run away from home again." And he hugged and kissed him. Just then in came mummy and guess what *she* had—*another* little gingerbread boy.

"This is your new brother," said daddy. "When you ran away and we couldn't find you I made *another* little gingerbread boy."

"Oh, how lovely! Now we can play together."

And so they did, and they all lived happy ever after.

Use these pages for your shopping list, starting with Silly Verse for Kids by Spike Milligan (7s. 6d.)